MW01065961

# Saint Thérèse of Lisieux

## Prayers & Devotions

by
Donal Anthony Foley

*All booklets are published thanks to the
generous support of the members of the
Catholic Truth Society*

  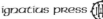

# Contents

# Origins and importance of the devotion

St Thérèse of Lisieux was born at Alençon in Normandy, in northern France, on 2nd January 1873, to Louis and Zélie Martin, the last of nine children. She lived a very hidden life in the Carmelite convent at Lisieux, entering at the early age of fifteen and dying when she was only twenty-four, in 1897. After her death, devotion to St Thérèse grew at a prodigious rate, and still, to this day, she is one of the most well-loved saints in the Church. She became posthumously famous particularly through her autobiography, *The Story of a Soul*, which was very influential, and also through her profound spirituality, that of the "Little Way", which seeks divine union not through rigorous mortifications, but by offering up small sacrifices and the sufferings of life to God in a spirit of self-oblation.

Many graces and miracles were obtained through her intercession, and she was beatified in 1923, and canonised by Pope Pius XI only two years later. Pope Pius X (1903-1914), had called her the greatest saint of modern times, an astonishing accolade for one who had lived such a hidden life.

*Thérèse's early years*

Her parents were very devout, and her father, Louis Martin, had wanted to become a religious, but this was not possible due to difficulties with his learning Latin. Instead, he settled on a career as a watchmaker. Zélie too had wanted to become a religious, but finally became a lacemaker. They met early in 1858, and married only three months later. Initially, they had decided to live a celibate or continent life together, but following advice from a priest, they embraced the marital state fully and eventually had nine children, of whom five daughters survived. Apart from Thérèse, three of her elder sisters, Marie, Pauline and Céline, became Carmelite nuns while the other sister, Léonie, became a Visitandine nun.

Both parents sought to pass on their strong Catholic faith to their children, who were brought up firmly, but with great love and affection. Thérèse, the youngest, was the particular favourite of her father, who called her his "little queen". Her parents attended daily Mass very early in the morning, observed the feasts and fasts of the Church, and prayed that one of their children would become a saint. In fact Louis and Zélie exhibited all the signs of sanctity themselves in the selfless manner in which they lived, and in the way they raised their large family. They were beatified at the behest of Pope Benedict XVI by Cardinal Jose Saraiva Martins, the papal legate, in October 2008, in the Basilica at Lisieux.

Thérèse was close to all her sisters, but particularly to Pauline, the second daughter, especially after the early death of their mother from breast cancer, in 1877, at the age of forty-five, when Thérèse was only four years old. Ultimately, when Thérèse entered the Carmel of Lisieux, Pauline was there to welcome her as prioress of the community. After Zélie's death, the family moved to Lisieux to be near Zélie's brother's family, the Guerins.

### Thérèse's life after the death of her mother

Thérèse was strong willed, even stubborn, as a young child, which was a cause of concern to her mother, so she was encouraged to make little sacrifices as a way of conquering self-will. After her mother's death, however, she became somewhat shy and withdrawn. The family, though, were very close, and the eldest daughter Marie tried to take the place of her mother as head of the household, even though she was only thirteen. It became Pauline's task to give the younger girls religious instruction, until she entered the Lisieux Carmel when Thérèse was nine. Her sisters' vocations stimulated a strong desire to emulate them, but Thérèse continued her education at the Benedictine convent of Notre-Dame-du-Pré, where she was not particularly happy due to some harassment from fellow pupils and her reserved nature.

The loss of Pauline to Carmel was a blow to Thérèse, and she became seriously ill, only recovering in May

1883, when a statue of the Blessed Virgin smiled at her. In Thérèse's own words, "Mary's face radiated kindness and love". In May 1885 Thérèse entered a period of scrupulosity for a year and a half, which was so trying that she later described it as a type of martyrdom. Marie entered Carmel in October 1886, and that Christmas, after midnight Mass, Thérèse reached a decisive turning point in her life. Thanks to a great grace, she was able to put her childhood fears behind her, and her sadness since the time of her mother's death, and devote herself completely to loving God. She later described this moment as her "conversion".

### Thérèse's entrance into the Lisieux Carmel

The next summer, in May 1887, when Thérèse was fourteen, she told her father that she too wanted to enter Carmel. He broke down in tears at this news, but recovered himself, and plucked a little white flower and gave it to her. She understood this was symbolic of her life, and how God had preserved her for himself.

She applied to Lisieux Carmel for entrance, but was refused because of her age. Later that year, however, Louis took Thérèse and her sister Céline on a pilgrimage to Rome. They arrived there on 20th November 1887, and were able to take part in a general audience with Pope Leo XIII. When Thérèse's turn came to approach the Pope, she knelt before him and asked the favour of being allowed to enter Carmel at the age of fifteen. He replied that she should do what the superiors decide, and that she would enter if it were God's will.

Events on the pilgrimage had taught her about the dangers of the world, from which she had hitherto been sheltered, and she returned to Lisieux more determined than ever to become a Carmelite. Finally, in April 1889, she was allowed to enter the Carmel, and became a postulant while only aged fifteen, taking the name Thérèse of the Child Jesus. She immediately felt a great sense of peace, a peace that in the main stayed with her to the end of her life, despite all the trials and difficulties she would have to endure. She adhered to the Carmelite rule with great exactness, and although her two eldest sisters were already installed in the Carmel, Thérèse deliberately kept her distance from them, denying herself the pleasure and support of their company, and generally only saw them during recreation.

### Thérèse's spiritual life deepens

She ended her postulancy in January 1889 and then became a novice, taking the brown Carmelite habit. From this point on, she tried to intensify her life of prayer, especially for priests, and to practise the virtues in numerous little ways. Thérèse also read the works of St John of the Cross, the great Carmelite reformer of the sixteenth century, deriving much benefit from them. She developed too, during her novitiate, a devotion to the Holy Face of Christ, that

face bruised and swollen during his Passion; and at the
ceremony of taking the veil, she added the words "and of
the Holy Face" to her name in religion, to become Thérèse
of the Child Jesus and of the Holy Face. Here in this name
we have a synthesis of the spiritual focus of her life: to be
humble and little, like the Child Jesus, but also to be one
with him in his sufferings. Finally, after a delay of eight
months because of her youth, she was able to make her
profession in September 1890, aged seventeen. During the
retreat before this event she underwent a period of spiritual
desolation, but afterwards regained her inner peace.

Meanwhile, in 1889, her father suffered a stroke, and
had to spend time in a private sanatorium. From this point
on, Thérèse further deepened her inner life, expressing it
outwardly in small acts and kindnesses, while accepting
any criticisms and unpleasantness directed at her. She also
focused more and more on the Gospels, as her spirituality
became simpler but more profound. But to most of her
fellow sisters, there seemed to be nothing outwardly
remarkable about her.

### *Thérèse's last years and death*

In February 1893, Thérèse's sister Pauline became prioress
of the Lisieux Carmel, and made Thérèse assistant to the
new novice mistress. As it happened, most of the work of
guiding the new novices fell to Thérèse, and she displayed
a rare talent for this.

Her father died in July 1894, and this allowed Céline also to enter the Lisieux Carmel. She brought her camera to the house, and this is the reason why we have so many fine photographs of St Thérèse. At the end of that year, as her sisters saw her health declining, they asked to her write about her childhood.

In June 1895, Thérèse wrote an Act of Oblation, which she and Céline read out before a statue of Our Lady. Later that year she began to correspond with a White Father, Fr Bellière, who asked for prayers and sacrifices to support his missionary work in Africa, and later with another priest, Fr Roulland of the Society of Foreign Missions, who made a similar request.

From this point on, her health steadily declined as the tuberculosis from which she suffered took its toll. At the end of Lent in 1896 she coughed up blood, and saw this as a sign that God would soon be calling her to himself. But it was to be more than a year before she actually died, and that was to be a period of progressively worse sufferings as the disease took hold.

In June 1897, her sister Pauline, now Mother Agnes of Jesus, asked Thérèse to write a further memoir focusing more on her religious life. Her sufferings, meanwhile, increased steadily, and as the end approached she said, "I would never have believed it was possible to suffer so much, never, never!" She died at the age of only twenty-four on 30th September 1897, her last words being, "My God, I love you!"

*The growth of devotion to St Thérèse after her death*

Thérèse's autobiography, which included selections from some of her poems and letters, was published after her death, with 2,000 copies being printed. This work stimulated interest in her life and gradually pilgrims began to visit her grave, as the first miracles due to her intercession were reported. The local bishop initiated her cause for canonisation in 1910, and this was taken up by Rome, under Pope Pius X. His successor, Pope Benedict XV, waived the requirement for the usual fifty-year delay between death and beatification because of the tremendous devotion to Thérèse that was already being displayed among Catholics. She was beatified in April 1923, by Pope Pius XI, and canonised by him in St Peter's Square, in May 1925, before a huge crowd. He also named her a Patroness of the Missions, and later on, in 1944, during Pope Pius XII's pontificate, she was named co-patroness of France, with Joan of Arc.

Since then, devotion to St Thérèse has continued to grow around the world, and in October 1997 Pope John Paul II, on the basis of the depth and profundity of the teaching upon which her Little Way is based, declared her a Doctor of the Church.

The major shrine dedicated to St Thérèse is the large basilica built in her honour in Lisieux. Work on it began in 1929, with the fulsome support of Pope Pius XI, and having been solemnly blessed by Cardinal Pacelli, the future Pope Pius XII, in July 1937, it was finally consecrated in 1951.

A good number of organisations devoted to spreading the message of St Thérèse, or which are under her patronage, exist in the Church, and there are also religious orders dedicated to her. The Little Way Sisters of St Thérèse was jointly founded by Archbishop Nicholas Mang Thang of Mandalay Archdiocese in Myanmar/Burma, and the late Miss Mary Doohan, the foundress of the Little Way Association, based in London.

A sign of the continuing extraordinary interest which St Thérèse generates can be seen in the way that her relics have toured the world in recent years. They were brought to England and Wales in the autumn of 2009, and large crowds turned out to venerate them in many churches and cathedrals.

### "Little Way" devotion of St Thérèse

Thérèse's spirituality has a number of striking characteristics, the most obvious being that unlike many of the great saints of the past, she lived a life without great outward asceticism. Similarly, she did not follow any of the traditional methods of meditation, but focused rather on simplicity and closeness to Christ. In addition, unlike the great saints of old, St Thérèse was not usually the recipient of any astounding spiritual favours: rather in her spiritual life she focused on profound contemplation, on seeking the gift of wisdom, on humility, and on her Little Way of love.

In this, she immersed herself completely in the idea that she was a child of the Heavenly Father, a child totally dependent on him for everything. She knew that little children do not try to do great things, but rather are content to do small acts for their parents, acts done with great love. One of her sayings was: "What matters in life is not great deeds, but great love."

St Thérèse also focused on the importance of humility, the virtue which makes us recognise our need for God's grace. She offered up many little acts of love to God, all the incidents, problems and difficulties of her life, no matter how small, and we know that she took her self-offering to the point of heroic virtue and sanctity.

*Thérèse's childlike spirit and acceptance of suffering*

The necessity of becoming like a little child in our relationship with God was strongly put by Jesus, after the disciples had asked him who was the greatest in the kingdom of heaven. In response, he called a little child to him and said, "Truly, I say to you, unless you turn and become like children, you will never enter the kingdom of heaven. Whoever humbles himself like this child, he is the greatest in the kingdom of heaven."

Thérèse, although she was not a child, possessed a childlike spirit, and her Little Way has also been described as a way of spiritual childhood, one that focuses on the simplicity and abandonment characteristic of a child who trusts its parents.

Regarding suffering, Thérèse made this rather disconcerting statement: "Sanctity lies not in saying beautiful things, or even in thinking them, or feeling them; it lies in truly being willing to suffer." As we have seen, Thérèse had much to suffer towards the end of her life, but abandoned herself completely to God saying: "I thank you, O my God, for all the graces you have bestowed on me, and particularly for having made me pass through the crucible of suffering." Shortly before she died she said: "Ah! to suffer in my soul, yes, I can suffer much." So while her sufferings were extremely painful, she accepted this pain in a spirit of love.

Ultimately, though, we have to remember that the way of Thérèse is a way of love and devotion, and that this love was the driving force of her life, expressed in a spirit of total abandonment to the will of God.

# Prayers and devotions to be said in front of the statue/icon

## Readings from Feast of St Thérèse

St Thérèse of the Child Jesus - 1st October

*Collect*

O God, who open your Kingdom
to those who are humble
and to little ones,
lead us to follow trustingly
in the little way of St Thérèse,
so that through her intercession
we may see your eternal
glory revealed.
Through our Lord Jesus Christ,
your Son, who lives and reigns with you
in the unity of the Holy Spirit,
one God, for ever and ever.

Isaiah 66:10-14

Now towards her I send flowing peace, like a river.
Rejoice, Jerusalem,
be glad for her, all you who love her!

Rejoice, rejoice for her,
all you who mourned her!
That you may be suckled, filled,
from her consoling breast,
that you may savour with delight
her glorious breasts.
For thus says the Lord:
Now towards her I send flowing
peace, like a river,
and like a stream in spate
the glory of the nations.
At her breast will her nurslings be carried
and fondled in her lap.
Like a son comforted by his mother
will I comfort you.
(And by Jerusalem you will be comforted.)
At the sight your heart will rejoice,
and your bones flourish like the grass.
To his servants the Lord will reveal his hand.

*Gospel* - Matthew 18:1-5

The disciples came to Jesus and said, "Who is the greatest in the kingdom of heaven?" So he called a little child to him and set the child in front of them. Then he said, "I tell you solemnly, unless you change and become like little children you will never enter the kingdom of heaven. And so, the one who makes himself as little as this little child is the greatest in the kingdom of heaven. Anyone who welcomes a little child like this in my name welcomes me."

## Litanies of St Thérèse

*Litany of St Thérèse I*

Lord, have mercy on us.
Christ, have mercy on us.
Lord, have mercy on us.
Christ, hear us.
Christ, graciously hear us.
God the Father of Heaven,
have mercy on us.
God the Son, Redeemer of the world, have mercy on us.
God the Holy Spirit, have mercy on us.
Holy Trinity, One God, have mercy on us.
Holy Mary, Mother of God, pray for us.
Our Lady of Victory, *pray for us.*
Our Lady of Mount Carmel,
St Thérèse of the Child Jesus,
St Thérèse of the Holy Face,
St Thérèse, spouse of Jesus,
St Thérèse, child of Mary,
St Thérèse, devoted to St Joseph,
St Thérèse, angel of innocence,
St Thérèse, model child,
St Thérèse, pattern of religious,
St Thérèse, flower of Carmel,

St Thérèse, zealous to save souls,
St Thérèse, converter of hardened hearts,
St Thérèse, healer of the diseased,
St Thérèse, filled with love for the Blessed Sacrament,
St Thérèse, filled with angelic fervour,
St Thérèse, filled with loyalty to the Holy Father,
St Thérèse, filled with a tender love for the Church,
St Thérèse, filled with extraordinary love for God
    and neighbour,
St Thérèse, wounded with a heavenly flame,
St Thérèse, victim of divine love,
St Thérèse, patient in sufferings,
St Thérèse, eager for humiliations,
St Thérèse, consumed with love of God,
St Thérèse, rapt in ecstasy,
St Thérèse, dedicated to pray for priests,
St Thérèse, who refused God nothing,
St Thérèse, who desired always to be as a little child,
St Thérèse, who taught the way of spiritual childhood,
St Thérèse, who gave perfect example of trust in God,
St Thérèse, whom Jesus filled with a desire for suffering,
St Thérèse, who found perfection in little things,
St Thérèse, who sought bitterness in this life,
St Thérèse, who told us to call you "little Thérèse",
St Thérèse, who gained countless souls for Christ,
St Thérèse, who promised after your death a shower
    of roses,

St Thérèse, who foretold:

"I will spend my Heaven doing good upon earth",
St Thérèse, Patroness of the Missions,
Lamb of God, who takes away the sins of the world,
spare us, O Lord.
Lamb of God, who takes away the sins of the world,
graciously hear us, O Lord.
Lamb of God, who takes away the sins of the world,
have mercy on us.

**V.** Pray for us, St Thérèse,
**R.** That we may be made worthy of the promises of Christ.

Let us pray

Hear our prayer, O Lord, we beseech you, as we venerate St Thérèse, your virgin and martyr of love longing to make you loved, and grant us, through her intercession, the gift of childlike simplicity and the spirit of complete dedication to your divine service. Amen.

### *Litany of St Thérèse II*

Lord, have mercy on us.
Christ, have mercy on us.
Lord, have mercy on us.
Christ, hear us.
Christ, graciously hear us.

God the Father of Heaven, have mercy on us.

God the Son, Redeemer of the world, have mercy on us.

God the Holy Spirit, have mercy on us.

Holy Trinity, One God, have mercy on us.

Holy Mary, *pray for us,*

Our Lady of Victory,

St Thérèse, servant of God,

St Thérèse, victim of the merciful love of God,

St Thérèse, spouse of Jesus,

St Thérèse, gift of Heaven,

St Thérèse, remarkable in childhood,

St Thérèse, an example of obedience,

St Thérèse, lover of the will of God,

St Thérèse, lover of peace,

St Thérèse, lover of patience,

St Thérèse, lover of gentleness,

St Thérèse, heroic in sacrifice,

St Thérèse, generous in forgiving,

St Thérèse, benefactress of the needy,

St Thérèse, lover of Jesus,

St Thérèse, devoted to the Holy Face,

St Thérèse, consumed with divine love of God,

St Thérèse, advocate of extreme cases.

St Thérèse, persevering in prayer,

St Thérèse, a powerful advocate with God,

St Thérèse, showering roses,

St Thérèse, doing good upon earth,

St Thérèse, answering all prayers,
St Thérèse, lover of holy chastity,
St Thérèse, lover of voluntary poverty,
St Thérèse, lover of obedience,
St Thérèse, burning with zeal for God's glory,
St Thérèse, inflamed with the Spirit of Love,
St Thérèse, child of benediction,
St Thérèse, perfect in simplicity,
St Thérèse, so remarkable for trust in God,
St Thérèse, gifted with unusual intelligence,
St Thérèse, never invoked without some answer,
St Thérèse, teaching us the sure way,
St Thérèse, victim of Divine Love,
Lamb of God, who takes away the sins of the world,
spare us, O Lord.
Lamb of God, who takes away the sins of the world,
graciously hear us, O Lord.
Lamb of God, who takes away the sins of the world,
have mercy on us.
St Thérèse, the Little Flower of Jesus, pray for us.

Let us pray

O God, who inflamed with your Spirit of Love the soul of
your servant Thérèse of the Child Jesus, grant that we may
also love you and may make you much loved.
Amen.

## Novenas to St Thérèse

*Twenty-four* Glory Be to the Fathers *Novena*

To carry out this Novena, one should say twenty-four *Glory Be's* each day for nine days in honour of the Holy Trinity, and in remembrance of the twenty-four years that St Thérèse of the Child Jesus lived. The following prayer can also be said before the *Glory Be's*:

Holy Trinity, God the Father, God the Son, and God the Holy Ghost, I thank you for all the blessings and favours you have showered upon the soul of your servant Thérèse of the Child Jesus, during the twenty-four years she spent here on earth, and in consideration of the merits of this your most beloved Saint, I beseech you to grant me this favour... if it is in accordance with your most holy will and is not an obstacle to my salvation.

This prayer can be said after each *Glory Be*:

St Thérèse of the Child Jesus, pray for us.

(*Glory be to the Father, and to the Son, and to the Holy Spirit, as it was in the beginning, is now, and ever shall be, world without end. Amen.*)

## A nine-day novena to St Thérèse[1]

Prayer to be said each day:

O St Thérèse of the Child Jesus, who during your short life on earth became a mirror of angelic purity, of love strong as death, and of wholehearted abandonment to God, now that you rejoice in the reward of your virtues, cast a glance of pity on me as I leave all things in your hands. Make my troubles your own, speak a word for me to Our Lady Immaculate, whose flower of special love you were - to that Queen of Heaven "who smiled on you at the dawn of life". Beg her as Queen of the Heart of Jesus to obtain for me her powerful intercession the grace I yearn for so ardently at this moment... and that she join with it a blessing that may strengthen me during life, defend me at the hour of death, and lead me straight on to a happy eternity. Amen.

O God, who did inflame with the Spirit of Love, the soul of your servant, Thérèse of the Child Jesus, grant that we also may love you and make you much loved. Amen.

First day:

O Thérèse of the Child Jesus, well beloved and full of charity, in union with you, I reverently adore the majesty of God, and since I rejoice with exceeding joy in the singular gifts of grace bestowed upon you during your life, and your

---

[1] from *http://www.carmeldundee.co.uk*.

gifts of glory after death, I give him deepest thanks for them; I beseech you with all my heart's devotion to be pleased to obtain for me (...*mention request here*). But if what I ask of you so earnestly does not tend to the glory of God and the greater good of my soul, do you, I pray, obtain for me that which is more profitable to both these ends. Amen.

St Thérèse of the Child Jesus, pray for us.

Second day:

Almighty God, giver of all good gifts, who did will that Blessed Thérèse, being watered by the heavenly dew of your guiding grace, should bloom in Carmel with the beauty of virginity and patience in suffering, grant that I your servant may go forward in the order of her sweetness and may be found worthy to become a devoted and loyal follower of Christ. Amen.

St Thérèse of the Child Jesus, pray for us.

Third day:

O Thérèse of the Child Jesus, lily of purity, ornament and glory of Carmel, I greet you, great Saint, seraph of divine love. I rejoice in the favours our Lord so liberally bestowed on you. In humility and confidence I ask you to help me, for I know God has given you love and pity as well as power. Tell him, now, I beseech you, of the favour I seek in this novena ... Your request will crown my petition with success and bring joy to my heart. Remember your promise to do good here on earth: "I shall spend my heaven doing good on the Earth. After death I shall let fall a shower of roses."

St Thérèse of the Child Jesus, pray for us.

Fourth day:

O Little Flower of Jesus, who at an early age had your heart set on Carmel and in your brief earthly life did become the mirror of angelic purity, of courageous love and of whole hearted surrender to Almighty God, turn your eyes of mercy upon me who trusts in you. Obtain for me the favour I seek in this novena ... and the grace to keep my heart and mind pure and clean. O dear Saint, grant me to feel in every need the power of your intercession; help to comfort me in all the bitterness of this life and especially at its end, that I may be worthy to share eternal happiness with you in heaven. Amen.

St Thérèse of the Child Jesus, pray for us.

Fifth day:

O Little Flower of Carmel, Almighty God endowed you, consumed by love for him, with wondrous spiritual strength to follow the way of perfection during the days of your short life. Sickness touched you early but you remained firm in faith and prayer was your life. O pray for me that I may benefit by your intercession and be granted the favour I ask in this novena...

St Thérèse of the Child Jesus, pray for us.

Sixth day:

O Little Flower of Jesus, you have shown yourself so powerful in your intercession, so tender and compassionate toward those who honour you and invoke you in suffering and distress, that I kneel at your feet with perfect confidence and beseech you most humbly and earnestly to take me under your protection in my present necessity and obtain for me the favour I ask in this novena ...Vouchsafe to recommend my request to Mary, the merciful Queen of Heaven, that she may plead my cause with you before the throne of Jesus, her divine Son. Cease not to intercede for me until my request is granted.

St Thérèse of the Child Jesus, pray for us.

Seventh day:

T hérèse of the Child Jesus, most loving Saint, in union with you I adore the divine Majesty. My heart is filled with joy at the remembrance of the marvellous favours with which God blessed your life on earth and of the great glory that came to you after death. In union with you, I praise God, and offer him my humble tribute of thanksgiving. I implore you to obtain for me, through your powerful intercession, the greatest of all blessings - that of living and dying in the state of grace. I also beg of you to secure for me the special favour I seek in this novena...

St Thérèse of the Child Jesus, pray for us.

Eighth day:

O glorious St Thérèse, who, burning with the desire of increasing the glory of God, invariably attended to the sanctification of your soul by the constant practice of prayer and charity so that, becoming in the Church a model of holiness, you are now in Heaven the protector of all those who have recourse to you in faith. Look down upon me who invokes your powerful patronage and join your petition to mine that I be granted the favour I seek in this novena...

St Thérèse of the Child Jesus, pray for us.

Ninth day:

O St Thérèse, seraphic virgin, beloved spouse of our crucified Lord, you who on earth did burn with a love so intense toward your God and my God, and now glow with a bright and purer flame in paradise, obtain for me, I beseech you, a spark of that same holy fire which shall help me to put things of the world in their proper place and live my life always conscious of the presence of God. As I conclude my novena I also beg of you to secure for me the special favour I seek at this time...

St Thérèse of the Child Jesus, pray for us.

## Prayers by St Thérèse

### *Morning offering*

O my God! I offer you all my actions of this day for the intentions and for the glory of the Sacred Heart of Jesus. I desire to sanctify every beat of my heart, my every thought, my simplest works, by uniting them to its infinite merits; and I wish to make reparation for my sins by casting them into the furnace of its merciful love. O my God! I ask of you for myself and for those whom I hold dear the grace to fulfil perfectly your holy will, to accept for love of you the joys and sorrows of this passing life, so that we may one day be united together in Heaven for all eternity. Amen.

### *Prayer to the Holy Child*

O little Jesus, my only treasure, I abandon myself to every one of your adorable whims. I seek no other joy than that of making you smile. Grant me the graces and the virtues of your holy childhood, so that on the day of my birth into Heaven the angels and saints may recognise in your little spouse ... Thérèse of the Child Jesus.

### *Prayer to the Holy Face*

O adorable Face of Jesus, sole beauty which ravishes my heart, vouchsafe to impress on my soul your divine likeness, so that it may not be possible for you to look at your spouse without beholding yourself. O my Beloved, for love of you I am content not to see here on earth the sweetness of your glance, nor to feel the ineffable kiss of your sacred lips, but I beg of you to inflame me with your love, so that it may consume me quickly, and that soon Thérèse of the Holy Face may behold your glorious countenance in Heaven.

### Prayer for humility

I implore you, dear Jesus, to send me a humiliation whenever I try to set myself above others. You know my weakness. Each morning I resolve to be humble, and in the evening I recognise that I have often been guilty of pride. The sight of these faults tempts me to discouragement; yet I know that discouragement is itself but a form of pride. I wish therefore, O my God, to build all my trust upon you. As you can do all things, deign to implant in my soul this virtue which I desire, and to obtain it from your infinite mercy I will often say to you: "Jesus, meek and humble of heart, make my heart like unto thine."

### St Thérèse's act of oblation

That my life may be one act of perfect love, I offer myself as a victim of holocaust to your merciful love, imploring you to consume me unceasingly, and to let the flood-tide of infinite tenderness, pent up in you, flow into my soul, so that I may become a very martyr of your love,

O my God. May this martyrdom, having first prepared me to appear before you, break life's thread at last, and may my soul take its flight unhindered to the eternal embrace of your merciful love. I desire, O my Beloved, at every heart beat to renew this oblation an infinite number of times till the shadows fade away and I can tell you my love eternally face to face.

### Act of oblation II

O my God, O Most Blessed Trinity, I desire to love you and to make you loved - to labour for the glory of your Church by saving souls here upon earth and by delivering those suffering in purgatory. I desire to fulfil perfectly your will, and to reach the degree of glory you have prepared for me in your kingdom. In a word, I wish to be holy, but, knowing how helpless I am, I beseech you, my God, to be yourself my holiness.

Since you have loved me so much as to give me your only-begotten son to be my saviour and my spouse, the infinite treasures of his merits are mine. I offer them gladly to you, and I beg to you to look on me through the eyes of Jesus, and in his Heart aflame with love. Moreover, I offer you all the merits of the saints in heaven and on earth, together with their acts of love, and those of the holy angels.

Lastly, I offer you, O Blessed Trinity, the love and the merits of the Blessed Virgin, my dearest Mother - to her

I commit this oblation, praying her to present it to you.
During the days of his life on earth her divine son, my
sweet spouse, spoke these words: "If you ask the Father
anything in my name, he will give it you." Therefore I am
certain you will grant my prayer.

O my God, I know that the more you wish to bestow,
the more you make us desire. In my heart I feel boundless
desires, and I confidently beseech you to take possession
of my soul. I cannot receive you in Holy Communion
as often as I should wish; but are you not all-powerful?
Abide in me as you do in the tabernacle - never abandon
your little victim. I long to console you for ungrateful
sinners, and I implore you to take from me all liberty to
cause you displeasure.

If through weakness I should chance to fall, may a
glance from your eyes straightway cleanse my soul, and
consume all my imperfections - as fire transforms all
things into itself. I thank you, O my God, for all the graces
you have granted me, especially for having purified me in
the crucible of suffering. At the Day of Judgment I shall
gaze with joy upon you, carrying your sceptre of the cross.
And since you have deigned to give me this precious cross
as my portion, I hope to be like unto you in paradise, and
to behold the sacred wounds of your Passion shine on my
glorified body.

After earth's exile I hope to possess you eternally, but I
do not seek to lay up treasures in heaven. I wish to labour

for your love alone - with the sole aim of pleasing you, of consoling your Sacred Heart, and of saving souls who will love you through eternity. When the evening of life comes, I shall stand before you with empty hands, because I do not ask you, my God, to take account of my works. All our good deeds are blemished in your eyes. I wish therefore to be robed with your own justice, and to receive from your love the everlasting gift of yourself.

I desire no other throne but you, O my Beloved! In your sight time is naught - "one day is a thousand years". You can in a single instant prepare me to appear before you. In order that my life may be one act of perfect love, I offer myself as a holocaust to your Merciful Love, imploring you to consume me unceasingly and to allow the floods of infinite tenderness gathered up in you to overflow into my soul, that so I may become a martyr of your love, O my God!

May this martyrdom one day release me from my earthly prison, after having prepared me to appear before you, and may my soul take its flight - without delay - into the eternal embrace of your merciful Love! O my Beloved, I desire at every beat of my heart to renew this oblation an infinite number of times, "till the shadows retire" and everlastingly I can tell you my love face to face.

## Prayers to St Thérèse

### *Prayer to St Thérèse*

O little St Thérèse of the Child Jesus, who, during your short life on earth became a mirror of angelic purity, of love strong as death, and of wholehearted abandonment to God, now that you rejoice in the reward of your virtues, cast a glance of pity on me as I leave all things in your hands. Make my troubles your own, speak a word for me to our Lady Immaculate, whose flower of special love you were - to that Queen of Heaven "who smiled on you at the dawn of life." Beg her as the Queen of the Heart of Jesus to obtain for me by her powerful intercession the grace I yearn for so ardently at this moment and that she join with it a blessing that may strengthen me during life. Defend me at the hour of death and lead me straight on to a happy eternity. Amen.

### *Invocation to St Thérèse*

O Glorious St Thérèse, whom Almighty God has raised up to aid and inspire the human family, I implore your Miraculous Intercession. You are so powerful in obtaining every need of body and spirit from the Heart of God. Holy Mother Church proclaims you "prodigy of miracles", "the greatest saint of modern times".

Now I fervently beseech you to answer my petition (*mention here ...*) and to carry out your promises of spending Heaven doing good on earth, of letting fall from Heaven a Shower of Roses. Little Flower, give me your childlike faith, to see the Face of God in the people and experiences of my life, and to love God with full confidence. St Thérèse, my Carmelite Sister, I will fulfil your plea "to be made known everywhere" and I will continue to lead others to Jesus through you. Amen.

### *Little Way prayer to St Thérèse*

O Little Thérèse of the Child Jesus, please pick a rose for me from the heavenly gardens and send it to me as a message of love. O little flower of Jesus, ask God today to grant the favours I now place with confidence in your hands (*mention your requests ...*). St Thérèse, help me to always believe, as you did, in God's great love for me, so that I might imitate your "Little Way" each day. Amen.

### *Prayer for missionaries*

St Thérèse of the Child Jesus, you who have been rightly proclaimed the Patroness of Catholic Missions throughout the world, remembering the burning desire which you did manifest here on earth to plant the cross of Christ on every shore and to preach the Gospel even to the consummation of the world, we implore you, according to your promise, to assist all priests and missionaries and the whole Church of God.

*To obtain graces through the intercession of St Thérèse*

O Eternal Father, who art in heaven, where you crown the merits of those who in this life serve you faithfully, for the sake of the most pure love your little daughter, St Thérèse of the Child Jesus, had for you, seeing that while on earth she always did your will, so as all but to bind you to give her whatever she desires, incline your ears to the petitions which she offers up to you on my behalf, and hear my prayers by granting me the grace I ask.

*Our Father, Hail Mary, Glory Be.*

### Prayer to the Father

O Father in Heaven, who, through St Thérèse of the Child Jesus, desire to remind the world of the merciful love that fills your heart and the childlike trust we should have in you, humbly we thank you for having crowned with such great glory your ever faithful child and for giving her wondrous power to bring unto you, day by day, innumerable souls who will praise you eternally. St Thérèse of the Child Jesus remember your promise to do good upon earth, shower down your roses on those who invoke you and obtain for us from God the graces we hope for from his infinite goodness. O St Thérèse of the Child Jesus, who have merited the title of Patroness of the Catholic Missions throughout the entire world, we beseech you, according to your promise, help priests, missionaries, and the whole Church. Amen.

### Prayer for spiritual childhood

O my sweet Jesus, give me the charity and simplicity of St Thérèse of the Child Jesus, whose mission in heaven is to make others love the good God as she loved him, and to teach souls her Little Way. Give me such longings that I may not rest until my heart loves God with all my strength, until I arrive at the spiritual childhood of the Little Flower of Jesus. Amen.

### Prayer for world peace

O St Thérèse, Little Flower of Jesus, who won universal confidence, obtain for all nations the blessing of fraternal union. Exert your wondrous influence over hearts, so that all the children of the great human family may unite in love of the same Father who is in Heaven. Teach nations and individuals the great law of evangelical charity which you so well understood and practised here below and continue so gloriously now that you are in Heaven. Lasting agreement being thus established between nations, the desire of the Vicar of Jesus Christ may be soon realised, that is, world peace as a fruit of justice and charity. Amen.

### Short prayer

O God, who didst inflame with your spirit of love the soul of St Thérèse of the Child Jesus, grant that we also may love you, and may make you much loved. Amen.

*Canticle to the Holy Face, composed by St Thérèse
of the Child Jesus and of the Holy Face*

Jesus, Your ineffable image
Is the star which guides my steps.
Ah, You know, Your sweet Face
Is for me Heaven on earth.
My love discovers the charms
Of Your Face adorned with tears.
I smile through my own tears
When I contemplate Your sorrows.

Oh! To console You I want
To live unknown on earth!
Your beauty, which You know how to veil,
Discloses for me all its mystery.
I would like to fly away to You!

Your Face is my only homeland.
It is my Kingdom of love.
It is my cheerful meadow.
Each day, my sweet sun.
It is the Lily of the Valley
Whose mysterious perfume
Consoles my exiled soul,
Making it taste the peace of Heaven.

It is my Rest, my Sweetness
And my melodious Lyre.
Your Face, O my Sweet Saviour,
Is the Divine Bouquet of Myrrh
I want to keep on my heart!

Your Face is my only wealth.
I ask for nothing more.
Hiding myself in it unceasingly,
I will resemble You, Jesus
Leave in me, the Divine Impress
Of Your features filled with sweetness,
And soon I'll become holy.
I shall draw hearts to You.

So that I may gather
A beautiful golden harvest,
Deign to set me aflame with Your Fire.
With Your adorned mouth,
Give me soon the Eternal Kiss!

## Meditations

### Meditation by St Thérèse

Then opening the Gospels, my eyes fell on these words: "Jesus, going up into a mountain, called unto him whom he would himself" (*Mk* 3:13). They threw a clear light upon the mystery of my vocation and of my entire life, and above all upon the favours which Our Lord has granted to my soul. He does not call those who are worthy, but those whom He will. As St. Paul says: "God will have mercy on whom he will have mercy. So then it is not of him that wills, nor of him that runs, but of God that shows mercy" (*Rm* 9:15-16).

I often asked myself why God had preferences, why all souls did not receive an equal measure of grace. I was filled with wonder when I saw extraordinary favours showered on great sinners like St Paul, St Augustine, St Mary Magdalene and many others, whom he forced, so to speak, to receive his grace. In reading the lives of the Saints I was surprised to see that there were certain privileged souls, whom Our Lord favoured from the cradle to the grave, allowing no obstacle in their path which might keep them from mounting towards him, permitting no sin to soil the spotless brightness of their baptismal robe. And again it puzzled me why so many poor savages should die without having even heard the name of God. Our Lord has deigned to explain this mystery to me. He showed me the book of nature, and I understood that every flower created by him is beautiful, that the brilliance of the rose and the whiteness of the lily do not lessen the perfume of the violet or the sweet simplicity of the daisy. I understood that if all the lowly flowers wished to be roses, nature would lose its springtide beauty, and the fields would no longer be enamelled with lovely hues.

And so it is in the world of souls, Our Lord's living garden.

He has been pleased to create great Saints who may be compared to the lily and the rose, but he has also created lesser ones, who must be content to be daisies or simple violets flowering at his feet, and whose mission it is to gladden his divine eyes when he deigns to look down on them. And the more gladly they do his will the greater is their perfection.

I understood this also, that God's love is made manifest as well in a simple soul which does not resist his grace as in one more highly endowed. In fact, the characteristic of love being self-abasement, if all souls resembled the holy doctors who have illuminated the Church, it seems that God in coming to them would not stoop low enough. But he has created the little child, who knows nothing and can but utter feeble cries, and the poor savage who has only the natural law to guide him, and it is to their hearts that he deigns to stoop. These are the field flowers whose simplicity charms him; and by his condescension to them Our Saviour shows his infinite greatness. As the sun shines both on the cedar and on the floweret, so the divine sun illumines every soul, great and small, and all correspond to his care - just as in nature the seasons are so disposed that on the appointed day the humblest daisy shall unfold its petals.

(From *The Story of a Soul*, Chapter 1, January 1895, First English translation by T.N.T. Taylor, 1926)

*Meditation on St Thérèse by Pope John Paul II in 1997*

The science of divine love, which the Father of mercies pours out through Jesus Christ in the Holy Spirit, is a gift granted to the little and the humble so that they may know and proclaim the secrets of the kingdom, hidden from the learned and the wise; for this reason Jesus rejoiced in the Holy Spirit, praising the Father who graciously willed it so (cf. *Lk* 10:21-22; *Mt* 11:25-26).

Mother Church also rejoices in noting that throughout history the Lord has continued to reveal himself to the little and the humble, enabling his chosen ones, through the Spirit who "searches everything, even the depths of God" (1 *Co* 2:10), to speak of the gifts "bestowed on us by God ... in words not taught by human wisdom but taught by the Spirit, interpreting spiritual truths in spiritual language" (1 *Co* 2:12, 13).

Shining brightly among the little ones to whom the secrets of the kingdom were revealed in a most special way is Thérèse of the Child Jesus and the Holy Face, a professed nun of the Order of Discalced Carmelites, the 100th anniversary of whose entry into the heavenly homeland occurs this year.

During her life Thérèse discovered "new lights, hidden and mysterious meanings" and received from the divine teacher that "science of love" which she then expressed with particular originality in her writings. This science is the luminous expression of her knowledge of the mystery of the kingdom and of her personal experience of grace. It can be considered a special charism of Gospel wisdom which Thérèse, like other saints and teachers of faith, attained in prayer.

The reception given to the example of her life and Gospel teaching in our century was quick, universal and constant. As if in imitation of her precocious spiritual maturity, her holiness was recognised by the Church in the space of a few years.

And so the spiritual radiance of Thérèse of the Child Jesus increased in the Church and spread throughout the world. Many institutes of consecrated life and ecclesial movements, especially in the young churches, chose her as their patron and teacher, taking their inspiration from her spiritual doctrine. Her message, often summarised in the so-called "Little way", which is nothing other than the Gospel way of holiness for all, was studied by theologians and experts in spirituality. Cathedrals, basilicas, shrines and churches throughout the world were built and dedicated to the Lord under the patronage of the Saint of Lisieux. The Catholic Church venerates her in the various Eastern and Western rites. Many of the faithful have been able to experience the power of her intercession. Many of those called to the priestly ministry or the consecrated life, especially in the missions and the cloister, attribute the divine grace of their vocation to her intercession and example.

The Pastors of the Church, beginning with my predecessors, the Supreme Pontiffs of this century, who held up her holiness as an example for all, also stressed that Thérèse is a teacher of the spiritual life with a doctrine both spiritual and profound, which she drew from the Gospel sources under the guidance of the divine teacher and then imparted to her brothers and sisters in the Church with the greatest effectiveness.

And so, a century after her death, Thérèse of the Child Jesus continues to be recognised as one of the great masters of the spiritual life in our time.

(Adapted from the Apostolic Letter of His Holiness Pope John Paul II, *Divini Amoris Scientia*, given on the occasion of St Thérèse of the Child Jesus and the Holy Face being proclaimed a Doctor of the Universal Church, on 19th October 1997.)

# TWO SISTERS IN THE SPIRIT
## Thérèse of Lisieux &
## Elizabeth of the Trinity

HANS URS VON BALTHASAR

This unique theological biography of two holy Carmelite sisters gives profound insights into their spirituality, showing that their differences actually complement one another. Hans Urs von Balthasar probes the depths of the contemplative mission of these young Carmelites, both of whom died in their twenties. Both women are clearly shown as daughters of their Carmelite heritage, but with their own unique outlooks.

*TSS-P... 499 pp., Paperback, $19.95*

ignatius.com • (800) 651-1531

# THE HIDDEN FACE
## A Study of St. Thérèse of Lisieux

### IDA FRIEDERIKE GÖRRES

This study of the life and character of St. Thérèse of Lisieux is a remarkable, penetrating, and fascinating search for the truth behind one of the most astounding religious figures of modern times. As objectively as possible, Görres presents the true Thérèse, revealing the stark drama within the cloistered world of the Carmel, the tension between personalities, and the daily details of conventual life—all throwing light on the tremendous purifying process that turned a pampered darling into a saint of heroic virtue.

*HFSST-P... 434 pp., Paperback, $19.95*

**ignatius.com • (800) 651-1531**

# INSPIRING TALKS
## THAT CHANGE LIVES

### THE HEALING POWER OF CONFESSION
Dr. Scott Hahn

Dr. Hahn presents the historical and biblical origins of the Sacrament of Reconciliation, providing an important guide for new Catholics and a source of renewal for "old hands".

### THE SECOND GREATEST STORY EVER TOLD
Fr. Michael Gaitley, M.I.C.

Fr. Gaitley describes a story that encompasses Divine Mercy, the life of St. John Paul II, and the crucial role that Marian Consecration can play in your life.

---

**OVER 300 CDs, BOOKS, BOOKLETS, & PAMPHLETS AVAILABLE**

Call **(866) 767-3155** to order
or visit **LighthouseCatholicMedia.org**

# LESSONS FROM A
# SPIRITUAL MASTER

## KNOWING THE LOVE OF GOD
### FR. REGINALD GARRIGOU-LAGRANGE, O.P.

In this collection of retreat talks, the beloved Fr. Garrigou-Lagrange gives us a blueprint for progress in the spiritual life. This book is permeated with rich doctrine and is ideal for devotional use. *Knowing the Love of God* will help those known and loved by God to know and love the same God.

**OVER 300 CDs, BOOKS, BOOKLETS, & PAMPHLETS AVAILABLE**

Call **(866) 767-3155** to order
or visit **LighthouseCatholicMedia.org**

Download the free
# CATHOLIC STUDY BIBLE APP
## IGNATIUS-LIGHTHOUSE EDITION

*A free digital version of the entire Bible (RSV-2CE)*

- Ignatius Study Bible notes and commentary available for purchase
- Dramatized audio New Testament* available for purchase (**FREE** audio of the Gospel of John)
- 10 hours of **FREE** audio commentary from Dr. Scott Hahn
- Over 200 Lighthouse talks available for purchase

\* Includes a foreword from Pope Emeritus Benedict XVI

**AVAILABLE FOR:**

 iPad iPhone iPod touch  Google play kindle fire

Search **CATHOLIC STUDY BIBLE** in the App Store